Dreams of
INDIA

ये चित्र समर्पित हैं मेरे भारत वासियों को
जिनके दर्शन में मैंने ये क्षण पाए
———— रघु राय ————

I would like to dedicate these images to the people of India, for they have blessed me with these moments.

———————————— Raghu Rai ————————————

DREAMS OF INDIA

First published in the United States of America 1988
by Collins Publishers Inc., San Francisco,
London, Glasgow, Toronto, Sydney, Auckland, Johannesburg.

© Copyright 1988 Times Editions
Times Editions
422 Thomson Road
Singapore 1129

Library of Congress Cataloging-in-Publication Data
Rai, Raghu, 1942-
Dreams of India.

1. India — Description and travel — 1981 — Views.
I. Title.
DS408.R35   1988   779'.95404   88-20400
ISBN 0-00-215165-0

Photographs by Raghu Rai
Cover photograph shot in India by Raghu Rai
Typesetting by Superskill, Singapore
Color separation by Far East Offset, West Malaysia
Printed by Mondadori, Italy
First printing October 1988
10 9 8 7 6 5 4 3 2 1

Pages 4-5: On its journey to the Bay of Bengal, the Ganga flows past the Maharajah of Benares' 17th century palace.

Pages 6-7: A 16th century hilltop palace and a cluster of medieval-looking mudbrick homes below dominate the city of Leh.

Pages 8-9: The vast desert state of Rajasthan is home to India's proud nomads with their legendary spirit of independence.

Pages 10-11: A young girl perched atop a roof patiently weaves a basket, oblivious to the majestic presence of Akbar the Great's palace complex at Fatehpur Sikri.

Dreams of
INDIA

RAGHU RAI

Introduction by
JOHN KENNETH GALBRAITH

Collins Publishers

INDIA AND THE ARTISTIC PERSONALITY

— John Kenneth Galbraith

In the spring of 1961, for many of us a rather sparkling moment in world history, I went to India. I had been appointed ambassador to that country by the new young President John F. Kennedy and, after some acrimonious but non-threatening dissent, the appointment was finally confirmed by the Senate. My diplomatic skills, which I chose to think accomplished, had not previously been a matter for notice or comment. My appointment was thought the result of a long and close association with the Kennedy family, young and old, and more particularly with J.F.K. There was truth in that supposition. But I had two and perhaps three other qualifications, one of which was an interest in Indian art that has led me here to this glowing book. Perhaps fortunately, there were a few more solemn ones or what were so considered.

On previous trips to India, including a three months' sojourn in 1956 when I was seeking to overcome a grave writer's block while working on the book that eventually became *The Affluent Society*, I had become aquainted with Jawaharlal Nehru and quite a few others of the senior Indian leaders. I had participated extensively in discussions of Indian economic development and, in fact, when I arrived as ambassador, Nehru greeted me with the rewarding hope that my new post would not rule me out as an unofficial adviser on Indian economic affairs. Few ambassadors have, I judge, been accorded so agreeable a greeting. My friendship with Nehru (and that of my wife) was the greatest of my advantages in the ensuing years. To be an ambassador serving between John F. Kennedy and Jawaharlal Nehru was, indeed, a privileged thing.

As an economist, I also had a presumed knowledge of the Indian economy. This was a lesser matter, and I do not dwell on it, for, as I later discovered, much of what I then believed was wrong. With others, I saw India as the natural beneficiary of the developed economic wisdom of the United States and the other industrial countries. What worked in industry, agriculture, technology and government policy and practice in the United States, as also in the other developed countries, could it was believed, be transferred without great modification to the Indian subcontinent. Alas, it was not so. India, one later learned, had to trace its own path to development. Before advanced industrial development could take place, there first must be smaller-scale enterprise. Before elaborate government guidance and planning could be implemented, there first must be the more elementary, less administratively demanding market economy. So too with agriculture. Not the diversely sophisticated models of Iowa or Illinois but a primary concern for seed (including new hybrids) and good soil and water management. Much of this, as noted, I had later to learn.

Finally I came to India knowing that on the world scene India had a separate and indeed unique personality — artistic and cultural. This is a matter of prime importance. It is something that is still imperfectly understood on a wide scale, a phenomenon on which I here wish to say a word.

There are some countries that have a shared artistic personality and though this may vary as to detail it is still very much a part of a larger expression. So it is in the United States and in Britain, France, Germany, Italy and for that matter, the Soviet Union. One does not, when journeying to these countries, go to museums to see something that is different. One goes to see variants on a larger theme. As with painting and sculpture, so it is with architecture, music and drama. Sometimes someone will say: "That is very American." Or "typically French or Russian." That is only to emphasize how exceptional it is that something departs from the common expression.

Indian art is not, however, a variant on a larger theme. The Indian artistic personality is its own. And not only is it India's own, but it is minute, spacious, complex, infinitely varied within the larger personality, and it reaches out over painting and sculpture to architecture, music, drama and the dance. One does not go to India to see variations on one's own world; one goes to India to visit a new and different world. This also is why Indians, when coming to the West, never quite separate themselves from their earlier culture. It explains the world-wide fascination with India, and accounts for the influence and even power that it exercises, far beyond anything served by diplomatic, military or economic achievement. This influence underlies, I think, the compelling appeal of these photographs of Indians and the Indian scene by a truly accomplished Indian artist.

My own experience of these matters — and few events are more strongly registered in my memory — dates from a pleasant early spring day in Benares in 1956, a full thirty-two years ago as I write.

I had given a lecture at Benares University, lunched with some members of the faculty, and, with my wife Catherine Galbraith, later very much an Indian scholar in her own right, was making a casual visit to the Bharat Kala Bhavan art museum. There, in room after room, I became fully aware for the first time of Indian painting, that of the Mughal courts and the often superb works from out in the provincial cities — provincial Mughal, as this style has since been characterized. And also the paintings of the princely courts of the Rajputs, some large but mostly very small, that emerged during the decline and disintegration of Mughal power and empire. Perhaps on that day, maybe later, I became aware of the painting that was done in the mostly minuscule courts in the Punjab hills and valleys bordering the Himalayas where artists took refuge, found employment, worked and discovered talented pupils in the declining years of Mughal rule. This painting remained largely unnoticed for a hundred years, until it was rediscovered by the great Indian art historian Ananda Coomaraswamy during the First World War.

Of this history I later became aware. On that day in Benares I was struck, indeed enchanted, by the delicacy of line in the paintings, the beauty and grace of the figures, especially of the women, the wonderful (but not always) gentle coloring and, perhaps most of all, the celebration of life that was depicted. This last is a matter to which I must return, for it is central, I think, to the distinct artistic personality of India.

Leaving Benares to return to Calcutta, I resolved to know more of this magical work — of these small paintings, often incorrectly called miniatures, which had so caught my attention. I began to search out the still limited literature on this subject, to assemble a small library (which has since been passed on to Smith College) and to search out scholars from whom I might have instruction. This study I continued in a deliberately serious way when I became ambassador.

The post of an ambassador someone once described as being rather like that of the pilot of an airplane: there are moments of panic and hours of boredom. My artistic concerns admirably occupied the latter hours. Prime Minister Nehru, who learned early of my interest, greatly approved; it indicated a commendable appreciation of Indian values — of the Indian artistic personality — and, perhaps, an equally commendable doubt as to the absolute validity of the Western technological and acquisitive culture.

In time, as my education continued, I had the happy chance to encounter Mohinder Singh Randhawa, and this led to an association which I remember with more pleasure than almost any other in my life. A superbly self-educated scholar — who passed into the rigidly exclusive Indian Civil Service (ICS) without having been to college — he was variously in life a leading civil servant, an innovative university president, the acknowledged authority on the history of Indian agriculture, the author of an important and lucid work on the history of science and the dean of Indian critics of art, on which subject he had written extensively and at the highest level of authority.

As my instruction on Indian painting from Randhawa (and my own reading) continued, we decided to write a book on the subject for a larger American and European audience. This we proceeded to do, and it came out to appreciative reviews in 1968 and which since has been variously republished. I have said that our book on Indian painting had very satisfactory reviews; it was also the only book of any importance that I ever wrote that did not attract political criticism or even forthright condemnation. Perhaps, I was led to think, I might with earlier wisdom have found a more tranquil life in the arts.

For me at least the strongest manifestation of the Indian artistic personality has been in painting and architecture, although this unquestionably reflects personal interest and competence. That others will find it in music and dance and now in the cinema or, as in this volume (and not for the first time), in photography, I do not doubt.

The separate personality in painting is manifest, first of all, in the motivating purpose. Western painting, as all recognize or assert, is the release of the inner expression of the artist. The painting of India yields far more to the perception and purpose of the patron. Nearly all of the good painting was done in the courts. There the painters, the denizens of the atelier, enjoyed a caste position more or less equal in status with that of carpenters. Western artists depicting court or religious figures — kings, dukes, cardinals — certainly knew whom they were to serve. But the Indian artists painted very specifically to give life to the daily activities of the court, its ruler and his women. Attention too was paid to his enjoyments, including especially his sports, notably hunting, and to the mystic life and beliefs which gave this pleasant existence its larger and deeper dimension.

To a marked extent, in fact, the painters of the atelier served the court as in a later age would the photographers. They were there to depict and immortalize the ruler, to inscribe for all time his position in history. Perhaps it was justly so that the names of all save the very greatest artists are unknown. Perhaps it could be said that they enlarged their scene by providing access to the imagination as do, I think, the pictures in this book. It is in keeping that when the camera arrived in India, the painting in the princely courts, already somewhat in decline, all but disappeared.

These matters — art as visual biography, pre-photographic history — set Indian painting apart, but so, more especially, does another feature of the Indian artistic personality. That is its commitment not to solemn or sober purpose but to wonderfully varied and relaxed enjoyments. Western painting from the Renaissance to our own time, although with several exceptions, is a serious business. In religion it depicts the grim procession of events from the Last Supper on to Calvary. Or it offers stern and solemn portraiture. It was somewhat of a surprise when the Impressionists showed handsomely attired Parisians out on a picnic.

The Indian artistic personality, in contrast, relishes and celebrates the pleasures of life. Krishna, the most favored of the gods, is normally seen frolicking with the cowgirls. Lovers are seen in an intimacy that removes all doubt and that for a long while kept many Indian paintings out of the public galleries. Kings and princes are shown in graceful and seemingly perpetual relaxation with their courts and their concubines. Or, in contrast, they are seen in peculiarly violent sport. Women, directed by their spouses, relax on a terrace or in a garden. I do not ever recall having seen an Indian painting of men and women grimly at work. Doubtless there are such, but not many artists at an Indian court would have thought to celebrate *The Gleaners*.

Indian painting, this manifestation of the Indian artistic personality, was not entirely without external influence. During the time of the Mughals, the Emperor Humayan, while in exile in Persia, was enthralled by the work of Persian artists and brought three of the greatest of them back to Delhi. Their work was strong and vivid and their influence enduring. Later, during the reign of Jahangir, Jesuit missionaries brought the work of French artists to his Indian capital. Many years ago, while idling for a few days in Florence, I spent my hours at Villa I Tatti, Berenson's house and estate just beyond the edge of the city. In his library I searched out a small number of volumes on Indian painting; on one such therein reproduced, Berenson had scribbled a note, "Some evidence here of Fontainebleau influence." It was the long arm of the Jesuits. It suggested, I think, not subordination of the Indian personality to the influence of the Europe but surprise that there was any influence at all.

I have said it is the delicacy of line and tracery, the sensitivity of color, the joy of scene, that mark and set apart the Indian painter and his work — and which comprise the essence of the Indian personality. As always, however, there is danger in too easy a generalization. There were marked differences between the painting of the Mughal courts, that of the princely courts of the Rajputs in western India and those in the valleys of the Punjab Hills in northwestern India. And even among the individual courts, large and small, there were further variations in style and expression.

Sometimes differences were marked. Thus, in the minute state of Basohli on a fertile plateau some two thousand feet above the Punjab Plain, Kirpal Pal, an enlightened ruler of the late seventeenth century, nurtured a style of painting that remains distinctive to this day: strong primary colors — red, yellow and blue — and human faces and figures, eyes in particular, in a wonderfully compelling distortion. There is nothing quite like it elsewhere in India or to my knowledge anywhere else in the world. It is proof that the Indian artistic personality, however separate, is not encased in any narrow stereotype.

But I must now turn for a word on what, for most people, is the most readily visible manifestation of the Indian artistic personality. That is architecture.

Once, while serving as ambassador, I was giving a commencement address in a large south Indian university and was caught up in a conflict not between town and gown but between the secular and the religious communities. Not far from the university is one of the largest Hindu temples of the Indian south. In the course of smoothing the dispute, I was initiated into one of the more minor orders of the Hindu faith. I was cheered by the thought that this was a sensible concession in the event that Hinduism has a valid view of salvation or that residence in the hereafter is decided in a democratic way, for there would be many Hindu voters. I was slightly depressed though by the thought that the transmigration of my soul might indeed bring me to live in something that is architecturally akin to this temple.

Hindu architecture as exemplified at Ranakpur in Rajasthan, one of the greatest and least visited treasures of the subcontinent, is a marvelous expression of the Indian artistic personality. And as in the case of the great black pagoda of Konarak on the eastern coast or the temples of Khajuraho in central India, it too celebrates the joys of life, including through its sculptures some extraordinarily imaginative designs depicting the act of love. Nevertheless, much Hindu architecture is heavy, dark and even dull. I believe almost everyone will agree that the true glory of India is in the Mughal and Mughal-influenced structures — tombs, forts, palaces — of northern and western India. These, the great cathedrals apart, are perhaps the greatest achievement ever of the artistic imagination. They express equally with painting the Indian artistic personality.

Once, in 1958, I journeyed to Samarkand in Central Asia in the Soviet Union to see one of the sources of this art. It was from here that the Mughals descended on India and, after conquering much of the country, wisely decided to stay. I was the only visitor to Samarkand that day and had the services of both the designated guides.

It was a wonderful excursion. I rejoiced in seeing, with much else, the Bibi-Khanum mosque which in my notes of the time I described as a "soaring domed structure with an entrance arch, smaller mosques to the side and minarets in the manner of the Taj," adding, alas, that of the minarets "only one survives." Like the Taj Mahal it celebrated great and here, commendably tolerant love. The woman in question was the most beautiful but not, according to legend, the most rigorously virtuous wives of the great Timur.

The Bibi-Khanum and the other monuments of Samarkand and Central Asia are clearly a source of India's architectural wonders and they in turn reflect Persian models and sources. But it is to India one now goes to see these wonders, for it was in India that they reached the apogee of their development. The notable examples, to mention but a few, are the Red Fort in Delhi, the Agra Fort at Fatehpur Sikri — that deserted but still perfectly surviving city built and then abandoned by Akbar — the palaces of Jaipur and Udaipur and, preceding them and towering above all, the Taj Mahal.

There were, as noted, foreign sources. But it is in India, enriched with Hindu influences (as in the enchanting combination of salmon red stone and marble tracery) and improved by much unidentified and unidentifiable imagination, that one has the supreme achievement. Here is architecture's highest expression of the Indian artistic personality.

But I do not, of course, confine that personality to painting and architecture alone. It is also wonderfully manifest in Indian sculpture, the sculpture which celebrates all but exclusively the joys of the Indian form and spirit. And there is Indian music, drama and dance, which I have already mentioned but on which, alas, I cannot claim any serious authority. But even these are not the end.

Some years ago a friend of mine, Clark Worswick, brought me a remarkable collection of photographs from India covering the work of Raja Lala Deen Dayal in the years 1884 to 1910. They celebrated the scene, people, life and social enjoyments of the court as well as the possessions of Sir Mahbub Ali Khan, the Nizam of Hyderabad. The photographs were subsequently published in a handsome book, which I proudly wrote the foreword. Needless to say, I think the photographs here offered of Raghu Rai are also superb — a matter on which I speak out of past experience though hardly from great authority. (Once many years ago, as an editor of *Fortune*, I consorted with, and bought the work of the great photographers of the Second World War generation — Alfred Eisenstadt, Margaret Bourke-White, and the remarkable but less known Ferno Jacobs, and others.)

I believe I can say with confidence that we here celebrate a new and yet further adornment of the Indian artistic personality.

When John Kenneth Galbraith was America's ambassador to India he aptly described it as a "functioning anarchy". Who but avowed anarchists would drive starving cattle from their Rajasthani droughtlands to the irrigated Punjab through the very heart of traffic-choked New Delhi?

The Republic Day Parade commemorates India's pride and independence every January 26. Here, along Delhi's central vista, folk dancers, musicians and elephants parade in an hour-long procession. On this day, thousands of Indians throng both sides of the vista to celebrate the occasion. *(Photo by Nitin Rai)*

A parade of modern weaponry rolls down the two-kilometer expanse of Raj Path
to celebrate India's independence. Celebrations take place in all state
capitals but are most spectacular in Delhi.

Originally a fertility festival, Holi now marks the passing of winter. On this
festive day, participants spray one another with colored water and powders. Here,
in Gujarat, these tribal boys and girls celebrate Holi by dancing, singing
and playing homemade flutes.

25

When Raghu Rai approached these Gujarati tribal women at a Holi festival, they raised their cotton saris to veil their faces.

A favorite Indian legend is the story of how the Hindu god Krishna chose his mate, Radha, from among female cowherds. This Rajasthani girl leads her cow with all the grace of Radha going to meet her love.

Here, a young Rajasthani woman is about to hang a swing during the Teej festival,
celebrating the end of the monsoon season.

A young Hindu woman prepares for a purifying ritual dip.

In a country as overcrowded as India, privacy is hard to come by — even more so
when thousands of villagers congregate in makeshift camps
like this one at a country fair.

Spiritual rituals at Benares include dips in the holy waters of the Ganga. Modesty is
a tradition among Hindu women, and many bathe fully dressed.
Afterwards, sarees are laid to dry on the sprawling sandbanks.

Against a backdrop of film stars from India's past, this contemporary starlet
prepares for her next role.

Granite bas–relief figures at Mahabalipuram are the work of 17th century
craftsmen of the Pallavan dynasty.

Jaipur, capital of Rajasthan, was founded in 1727 by warrior-astrologer Raja Jai
Singh II. Frescoes march along the walls of ordinary homes, blending with the
city's everyday life to form scenes like classical miniature paintings.

Monkeys taking milk from complacent cows would appear out of place anywhere but India, where both are deified by the Hindu religion. These were photographed near Jaipur.

Vignettes of village life abound in the stone carvings of Mahabalipuram. In surrounding villages, long-horned cows are still milked by hand.

The Gwalior fortress in Madhya Pradesh state is three kilometers long and 1,000 years old. Images of Jain saints — the ascetic religion that inspired Mahatma Gandhi to non-violence — decorate the cliffs.

The sundial of Delhi's sculptural observatory, Jantar Mantar, is said to be accurate to within half a second. Designed in 1724 by a Rajput prince, the observatory also contains staircases "leading to the planets and the stars."

Visitors to Fatehpur Sikri perch themselves on top of the five-story Panch Mahal
Palace for lunch and a panoramic view. The palace complex is one of
India's most perfectly preserved landmarks.

The inlaid marble and carved ivory designs on this monument from the Mughal dynasty were crafted by ancient artists from Turkey, Persia and India.

A guide at the palace complex of the Mughal ruler Akbar in Fatehpur Sikri is
framed by intricate wall carvings. The word Fatehpur, meaning "City of Victory,"
was added to the settlement's name by Akbar to celebrate the success
of a major military campaign.

The Mysore palace, completed in 1912, contains stained glass from Scotland and solid silver doors. Its predecessor was destroyed in the late 19th century because its owner, the maharajah, simply tired of it.

Although child marriages and dowries are forbidden by law, both traditions remain popular. These young brides-to-be in Rajasthan, all members of one family, will share the costs of a multiple wedding celebration.

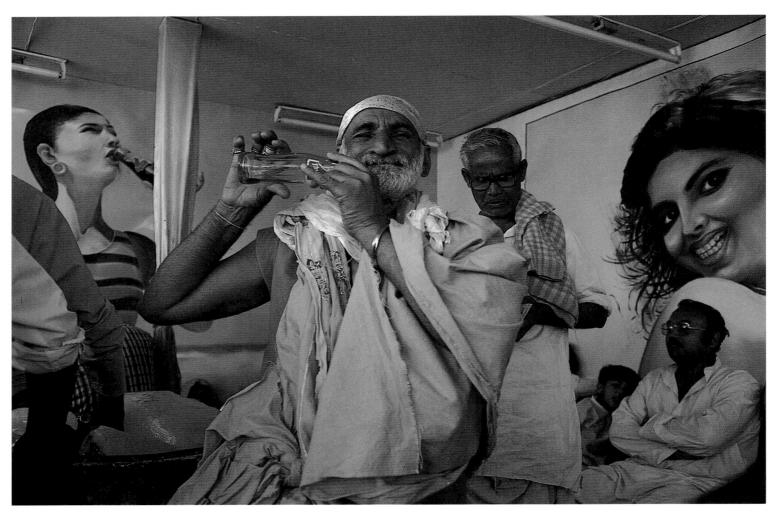

"Things go better with Coke" — or , in India, with the local favorite, Thumbs Up!
Here, a holy wanderer mimes a tune in a Himalayan meeting place.

These sidewalk salesmen in mountainous Kashmir have little time to sell their
wares because of bad weather and short tourist seasons.

Somber looks belie the reason these two Rajasthani teenagers are dressed so
colorfully — a wedding.

This poised nine–year–old bride poses while her eleven–year–old husband
clutches his ceremonial Rajput sword.

Marriages aren't made in heaven in India. For the urban middle classes, they begin
in the advertising columns of newspapers; in the villages, through the local barber
or marriage brokers. This Rajput bridegroom balances an ancestral sword — a
symbol of his family's martial past — across his knee.

Modern, egalitarian laws have decreased the status and wealth of India's maharajahs and reduced many of their opulent 19th century palaces to white elephants like this palace in Jaipur, draped in shrouds to mourn a passing era.

At the Dharamsala bazaar in mountainous Himachal Pradesh, a classical Indian
flute player creates another world that is all his own.

59

On the Yamuna River near the Taj Mahal, a hot-air balloon is prepared for an ascent.

Madhya Pradesh's Mandu, the "City of Joy," contains a number of palaces and
lakes, groves and gardens in the style of the great Mughals. The capital of the
Muslim Malwa kingdom in the 14th – 15th centuries, it is the largest fortified city
in the world with 75 kilometers of encircling walls.

A woman's bright yellow sari clashes beautifully with fuchsia flowers in a
doorway of the ancient Mughal palace complex at Fatehpur Sikri.

India's largest state, Madhya Pradesh, is homeland to 40 percent of the country's
tribal people. Here celebrators link in a foot-stomping dance traditional
to the spring festival of Holi.

Young women dressed in colorful saris wait for the Prime Minister to arrive to
open the Asian Games in Delhi. A white pigeon, symbol of peace, waits on the dais.

Contrary to its image, not all of Rajasthan is sand, camels and vividly dressed
nomads. From the terrace of the Siliserh Palace Hotel, spring unfolds a panorama
of crops sprouting from rich soil. In autumn, after the monsoons, the vista
is a shallow lake alive with water fowl.

A continuous flow of Indian tourists passes through the 54-meter tall Gate of
Victory to visit Jami Masjid mosque at Fatehpur Sikri. Here women pray for
fertility at the tomb of a Sufi saint who predicted the birth of
three sons to the Mughal emperor Akbar.

India abounds in tombs of Sufi saints like this one which draws worshipers from
all religions and from different parts of India.

A man balances a large basket on his head along the banks of an estuary in the Sunderbans southeast of Calcutta. A wildlife sanctuary, the area is home to Bengal tigers and some of the world's largest crocodiles.

A boatman gazes at a figure on the shore of the Ganga. Despite the belief by many
that the river has the power of self-purification, the government has enacted a $250
million program to combat the modern problem of pollution.

A wintry morning on the Ganga is warmed by a cup of strongly brewed
Himalayan tea, or *chai*.

A boulder balanced precariously amid other granite formations near Hyderabad
takes on a surreal quality in the glow of a sunset.

An enormous boulder and the outline of a sitar, one of India's native musical instruments, combine to create a study in symmetry on a pastoral landscape.

Laborers take a break from construction of a Sikh temple near Sirhind in the Punjab.

Sikhism was founded as a pacifist religion by Guru Nanak in the early 16th century, but within two centuries Sikhs were embroiled in politics. Their last guru, Gobind Singh, decreed that the faithful should always be armed and on the alert to defend their faith.

A *saddhu* should never be asked where he is from or where he's going. Since they
vow to be eternally wandering hermits, those facts are irrelevant. Some
travel alone, some in groups; some take vows of silence while
others preach or chant mantras.

In the changing times of India, this maharajah may have lost his power and wealth,
but his princely bearing and costume still command respect.

Resplendent in gold embroidery, this member of the Gwalior royal family stands
poised to confer a shawl on a bridal party. Notice the gold-handled sword in hand
and the distinctive *pagri*, or turban, perched jauntily on his head.

Every Hindu child is familiar with the epic *Ramayana*, which depicts the heroic deeds of Rama and the monkey-god Hanuman. At Hardwar, a pilgrim displays tattoos meant to honor the mythical twosome.

A widower poses beside a shrine to his deceased wife, complete with mementos
of their life together.

Today the Maharajah of Gwalior still lives in a part of the early 19th century family palace. Tourists marvel at the eccentricities like a cut-glass rocking chair, a room full of erotica and a silver model railway that distributes after-dinner brandy and cigars.

This tribal ruler from Madhya Pradesh has scarcely changed his way of life since
his forebears repelled Mughal invaders from the north three centuries ago. With
his curved sword and handlebar moustache he remains every inch the chief.

When crops fail, villagers drift to the cities and usually end up doing manual labor,
like this Rajasthani couple that whitewashes houses for a living.

The birthplace of two of the world's major religions, Buddhism and Hinduism,
India has a widely varied religious history. Shown here, worshipers
gather to express their faith.

Two timeless expressions of India's creativity: a village sculpted from mudbrick and the Taj Mahal. An ethereal mausoleum, the Taj commemorates the perfect love of Emperor Shah Jahan for his dead empress.

In its heyday, Patna was one of the world's largest cities, and the capital of the mighty Mauryan empire. It was here that two of India's gentlest religions — Buddhism and Jainism — took root.

The silhouettes of two men on a rooftop and a bird in a weather-ravaged tree
slowly fade to black as the sun sets on Dharamsala in the western Himalayan foothills.

Mahabalipuram, an idyllic seaside town, was originally named for King Mamalla, first royal builder of shrines and temples. Today, almost 70 monuments draw worshipers to this ancient site.

A roadside vendor fills another balloon with air for his makeshift shooting gallery, while the sun sets on Bombay in the background. Each day, three hundred families migrate to the city, and it is predicted that the population will double to 16 million by the year 2000.

When the Dalai Lama fled his native Tibet for India in 1959, nearly 100,000 of his
people followed. The Indian government provided land for settlements and now
the immigrants grow barley and maize, keep dairy herds and weave
carpets to supplement their income.

The central Himalayan region of Tehri–Garhwal has been pilgrimage country to Hindus since time immemorial. For a few rupees shelter can be found at a hostel–like *dharamsala* and daily visits made to pray at nearby temples.

In the old days, maharajahs kept fleets of Rolls Royces and private armies. But following the marriage of the daughter of the Maharajah of Scindia and the son of the Maharajah of Jammu-Kashmir, the wedding party rode through Gwalior in an open jeep.

Sikh women are strong, spirited, often enchanting and prefer to bow only to their holy book, the *Granth Sahib*, even though Sikh men are known for their aggressive approach to life — from their high profile in India's army to their agricultural successes in Punjab's "Green Revolution".

India of the '80s is symbolized by computers and technocrats communicating in big-business jargon. During Rajiv Gandhi's era, a yuppie generation has grown accustomed to a combination of designer jeans and traditional apparel, as modeled here.

Two generations await treatment at one of Mother Teresa's Missionaries of Charity.

India's maharajahs once entertained European royalty and the ruling Raj with tiger
shoots, horseracing and banquets served on silver and gold. In spite of reforms that
have reduced their power and prestige, some princely families still display
opulent gems at traditional celebrations.

As in a flashback to the days of princely rule, these landowners (or *jahgirdars*) sit deferentially through the birthday celebration of their maharajah. Feudal loyalty to the maharajahs still exists, despite the removal of their official titles and influence.

The stoic and introspective nature of much of Indian culture seems reflected
in the faces of these men.

For centuries, north India was trampled by a succession of invading armies who left a legacy of Aryan blood in their wake. In 326 BC the troops of Alexander the Great marched into Himachal Pradesh state, and even today, green and blue eyes, uncharacteristic in other parts of India, often typify the people of this region.

This Rajasthani brother and sister are two of the many artists, folk dancers and
singers who contributed to the Festival of India which toured
the U.S. and France in 1985.

Although modern India has made technological and social progress, the soul of the
vast subcontinent remains in her villages — many still without access roads and
less than half linked with electricity. Here villagers live with doors that are always
open — even to their ambling sacred cows.

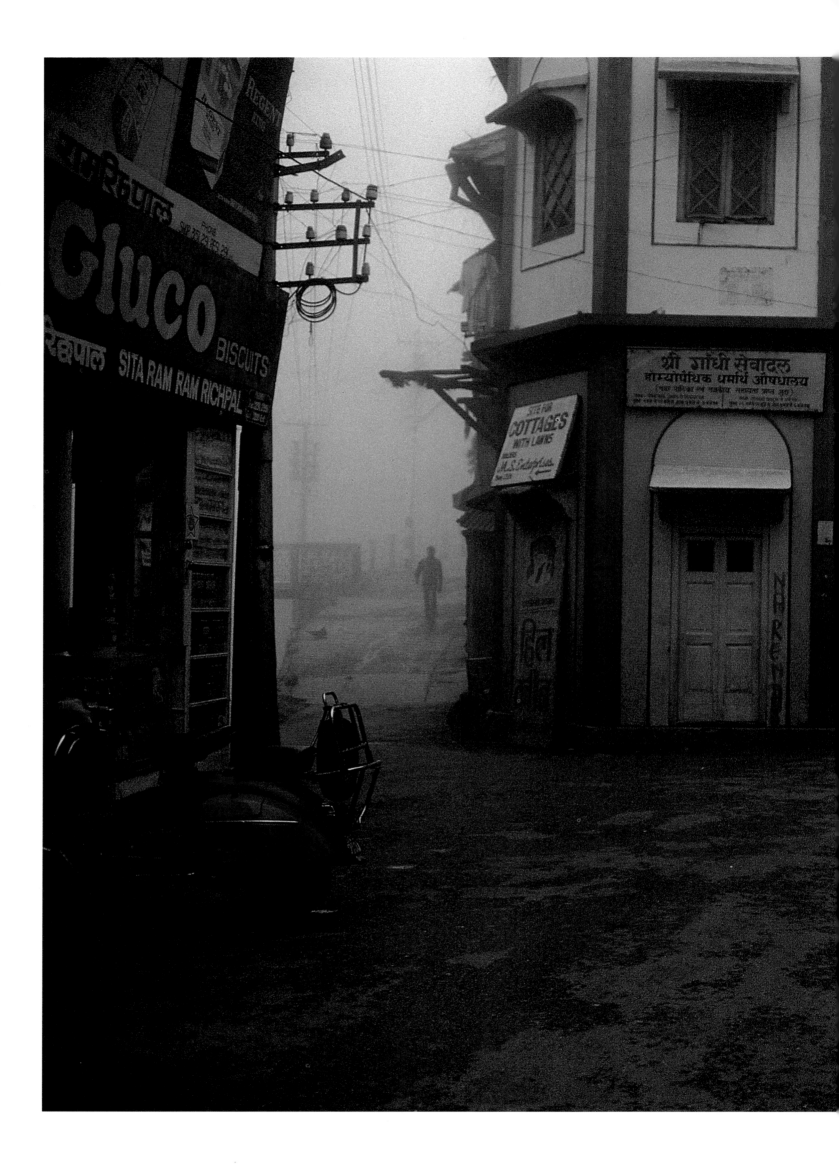

Hill stations were an invention of the mid–Victorian British, longing for the misty
cool of home. Most famous were Darjeeling and Simla, but smaller retreats like
this one, Mussoorie in Uttar Pradesh state, still provide cozy hotels and bracing air
to invigorate lethargic visitors.

In the ancient sandstone city of Jaisalmer, prosperous 18th century merchants vied
with rivals to build the most beautiful city mansions or *havelis*. The local craftsmen
created such exquisite designs for balconies, porticos and doorways that
Jaisalmer's *havelis* were listed as national treasures.

Here, a child gets a taste of an antiquated folk remedy — milk straight from the goat — said to be a good restorative. Also, the breath of goats has been thought to cure tuberculosis, so patients in rural areas sometimes sleep in the goats' pen.

No high-class Indian celebration is complete without painted elephants. Today,
the small-eared Asian elephants that once carried princes are more at home
transporting tourists through the long grass of wildlife parks.

The Indian Army participates in the Republic Day Parade at Lutyens, marching
from the Central Secretariat to India Gate.

A child in military dress appears to direct traffic for a turban-clad brass band.

India's military forces have progressed from curved scimitars and camels to nuclear-powered submarines and other modern weaponry. When an uproar resulted among Western nations over reports that India was developing nuclear arms, the country began purchasing military goods from the Soviet Union.

Tea time is a custom held over from India's British past, and these army troops
aren't letting frigid mountaintop temperatures prevent them from indulging
in an afternoon outdoor snack.

Amritsar is the holy city for Sikhs, and their marble and glided temple is a
sanctuary for all they revere. An earlier temple was sacked and rebuilt in 1764, and
the casing of copper plates overlaid with 400 kilograms of gold leaf was added later
by Maharajah Ranjit Singh, Lion of the Punjab and King of the Sikhs.

Sikhs both rich and poor, young and old, dedicate themselves to the task of removing silt from the holy tank around the Golden Temple at Amritsar — restoring it to the pristine "pool of nectar" from which the historic city takes its name. On this occasion Sikh priests recite special prayers from the holy book, *Granth Sahib*, around the clock.

Sikh men show loyalty to their clan and community by wearing distinctive
turbans and growing beards.

Every 12 years devoted Jains travel to Sravanabelagola in south India to witness the ritual cleansing of the 1000-year-old granite statue of Lord Gomateswara. Jainism was founded around 500 BC by Mahavira, a contemporary of Gautama Buddha.

Muslim faithfuls gather at Delhi's Jama Masjid mosque. Eleven centuries old,
Islam is India's second largest religion, with more than 80 million devotees.

A Brahmin priest distributes *prasad*, or holy food, to eager Hindus at the
Maharajah of Jaipur's temple in Rajasthan. The priests and teachers of Hindu India,
Brahmins constitute the highest caste in the country's well-defined social hierarchy.

This woman resting outside her farmhouse in the northwestern state of Himachal
Pradesh seems less than willing to be photographed, but her young
companion's face is full of curiosity.

These schoolchildren get a break from the confinement of the classroom and
continue their studies outdoors. Language can be complicated in India, where
1,652 languages are spoken and 15 appear on the country's currency, the rupee.

Nowhere illustrates India's curious urban juxtapositions better than Bombay: old
and new cultures existing in tandem; the very rich counting the very poor among
their neighbors. Often described as the New York of India, Bombay is India's
second most populous city and its economic center. Its vibrant cultural life reflects
a cosmopolitan and widely varied population.

The beauty of Rajasthan's capital, Jaipur, is viewed from the rooftop of an old
haveli, or city mansion. Jaipur's royal family is descended from warrior–astrologer
Jai Singh II, who built the city in 1727 to his astrological fancies.

The 13th century Sun Temple at Konarak was built as a gigantic stone chariot for
the sun god, Surya. The temple stands on a platform of 24 sculpted wheels
symbolizing the Hindu cycle of rebirth.

A Brahmin priest prepares for the daily *puja*, or offerings ritual, while the symbolic
statue of a bull seems to watch intently.

To India's 500 million Hindus, the mountains to the north are the sacred abode of
the gods. One of the most revered sites is Hardwar in Uttar Pradesh state, where
the faithful cleanse themselves of sin and congregate in the courtyards
of *dharamsalas*, or lodging places.

Where the Ganga and Yamuna rivers meet at Allahabad, Indians cleanse
themselves of sin in the holy waters and congregate for more mundane matters like
socializing. The ashes of Indian leader Jawaharlal Nehru were scattered in 1964 at
this site in the Uttar Pradesh state.

As long shadows engulf a street of bricks near a Sikh temple, a woman prays while
a grey-bearded Sikh smiles for the camera.

With trident in hand and consort Parvati at his feet, a statue of the Hindu god Lord
Shiva stands guard on the shore of the Ganga at Calcutta.

These Rajasthanis, more accustomed to dust storms than flash floods, watch as
heavy rains turn their desert into an oasis.

Pilgrims convene a colorful picnic near Agra's Red Fort in Uttar Pradesh state.
The fort was built in 1565.

A volunteer bucket-brigade of members of the religious sect called Radha-Swami,
an offshoot of Sikhism, moves earth and other materials to build a charity hospital.

In Rajasthan, the ancient fort Jaisalmer, completed in 1156, now serves as a sunny
spot for students to read their texts. In antiquity, the hilltop fortress guarded the
caravan route between the Middle East and Central Asia.

A young Ladakh boy is dwarfed by an immense windswept valley characteristic
of India's Himalayan terrain. The hardy inhabitants of this desolate area survive the
long winters on a simple diet of *tsampa* — roasted barley flour — and
dried vegetables and meat.

Firewood and other supplies are stored on the flat roofs of Ladakh in preparation
for severe winters that turn the moonscape-like plateaus into seas of snow and ice.

On her portico overlooking a stone quarry, a Rajasthani woman seems
preoccupied with something other than the view.

The opulent architecture of Mughal India in Fatehpur Sikri stands in stark contrast
to a vegetable farmer's simple mudbrick home.

Sunlight and shadows chase each other across the mountain desert of Ladakh, historically a part of Greater Tibet, while homesteads and Buddhist monasteries dot the landscape.

Ceremonial music played by a Tibetan Buddhist monk on his *gyaling* signals the
spring thaw in Ladakh, elevation: 4,500 meters, while a pair of *dzos* pull a wooden
plow through the half-frozen earth.

Symbolic offerings are made on the banks of the Ganga at Calcutta. The city is
named for the goddess Kali — a wrathful black-faced Hindu deity. At her riverside
temple, thieves once prayed for guidance before setting out in search of victims.

171

A fitness instructor straightens a student's pose during a fog-shrouded early
morning class at the Maidan, a Calcutta park.

Rajasthan's annual Pushkar camel fair draws 200,000 people and 50,000 "ships of the desert" for some spirited Middle Eastern horsetrading.

Smoke fills the air at a campsite of Rajasthan tribal people during the Pushkar
camel-selling festival, while the "beasts of burden" relax before the trading begins.

Pilgrims huddle and socialize during the mid–summer Rath Yatra festival in
Orissa, where they will ask the Hindu god Lord Jagannath to release them from
the cycle of rebirth. The word "juggernaut" was coined from the chariot of the
Hindu god because legend has it that devotees threw themselves under its wheels.

As laundry is washed and laid out to dry on the shore of the Yamuna River at Delhi,
bicyclists, automobiles and other vehicles flow across Boat Bridge in a steady stream.

Even thick fog can't dampen soapbox oratory among this group of Bengalis
in Calcutta's Maidan park.

Rough-hewn timbers lashed together for makeshift vessels add an eerie quality to
this southern beach bathed in the incandescence of a pink and orange sunset.

Under the threatening clouds of a monsoon sky, modern spotlights punctuate the purple glow surrounding the Taj Mahal.

The elaborate outline of Delhi's Jama Masjid mosque stands out against the onset of darkness on the evening of Id-ul-Fitr — the end of Islam's Ramadan month of fasting. India's largest mosque, its elaborate architecture is typical of ancient Mughal culture.

INDEX

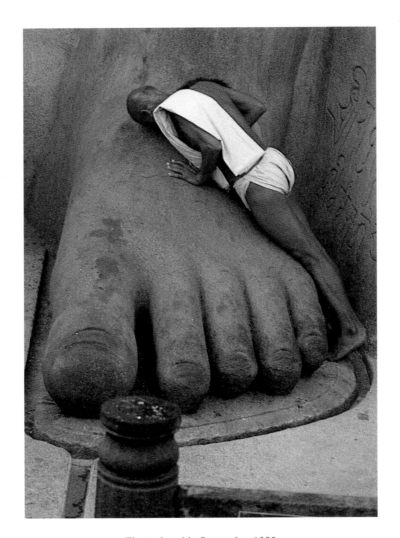

First printed in September 1988
Printed in Italy by A. Mondadori Editore, Verona